JULES MASSENET

MÉDITATION

(Thaïs)

Violin and Piano

Edited and arranged by
Herausgegeben und bearbeitet von
Roger Nichols

EDITION PETERS

LONDON · FRANKFURT/M. · LEIPZIG · NEW YORK

PREFACE

Thaïs, Massenet's tenth completed opera, had its première at the Paris Opéra on 16 March 1894 with the American soprano Sibyl Sanderson in the title role. The libretto by Louis Gallet was based on Anatole France's novel of the same name, serialized in the *Revue des deux mondes* in 1889 and published in book form the following year.

The story tells of the conversion to Christianity of the courtesan Thaïs by the holy man Athanaël (Paphnuce in France's novel), and of his parallel but opposite conversion to a life dominated by lust for her. The 'Méditation' for solo violin and orchestra, joining the two scenes of Act II, describes the beginning of Thaïs's conversion.

The work was not received well initially: by 1897, when Sanderson retired, it had reached only its fourteenth performance. But the 'Méditation' was an instant success with violinists, and its religious association also encouraged church organists to play it at Mass during the Communion. Even Pope Pius X's *motu proprio* of 1903, specifically demanding that the music heard in church should 'not include reminiscences of themes employed in the opera house', could not prevail against it.

Sources

There are five sources:

S sketches for the opera (BN. Mus. Ms 4232 (I, II)); those for the 'Méditation' are found in ff. 55–60

A autograph full score (Opéra A. 665. a. I–IV Rés.); II, ff. 430–447

EF first edition of the full score, Heugel, 1894, H. et Cie. 9434 (BN. Mus. Vm2 1029); pp. 277–289

EV first edition of the vocal score, Heugel, 1894, H. et Cie. 7644 (BN. Mus. Vmb 33); pp. 127–131

T transcription for violin and piano by Martin Marsick, Heugel, 1894, H. et Cie. 9625 (1d)

The sketches (S) are very close to the final version. In the present edition the few variants are noted simply as points of interest.

The autograph full score (A) and the printed full score (EF) together contain most of the main changes I have made to the established transcription (T). As the vocal score (EV) demands the compression of three staves onto two, it can be regarded only as a secondary source. As well as providing violin fingerings, phrasing, piano pedalling and verbal instructions, A and EF suggest two important modifications. Firstly, Marsick has consistently removed the final harp quaver in bars 1–8, 11–16 etc. I had a few qualms about restoring these, if only because in 1894 Marsick and Massenet were Conservatoire colleagues and presumably Marsick's transcription was overseen by the composer. But the removal of the quaver produces such an ugly hiccup in the texture that it seemed preferable to follow the text in A and EF (and EV), even if this calls for some mild agility from the pianist. Secondly, the return of the tune at bar 40 and the coda at bar 59 are accompanied in A and EF by a four-part chorus humming quietly, and in both sources the composer's instruction reads 'if voices are not available, <u>strings will play the small notes</u>'. Clearly he was determined on a change of colour in the accompaniment at this point. The present edition therefore includes the voice parts in small notes in bars 40–47 and again in bars 59–65, so that pianists can make this change of colour if they want to.

The bowing and fingering in the violin part are taken from A. The piano pedalling is editorial in bars 13–18, 25–37, 51–55 and 68–71. In all other places it follows T, except where noted in the Critical Commentary.

Roger Nichols

PRÉFACE

Thaïs, le dixième opéra achevé de Massenet, fut créé à l'Opéra de Paris le 16 mars 1894, avec la soprano américaine Sibyl Sanderson dans le rôle-titre. Le livret de Louis Gallet est fondé sur le roman du même titre d'Anatole France, publié en feuilleton dans la *Revue des deux mondes* en 1889 et sous forme de livre l'année suivante.

L'histoire raconte la conversion au christianisme, par Athanaël (Paphnuce dans le roman de France), de la courtisane Thaïs, et la conversion parallèle, mais conflictuelle, du saint homme à une vie dominée par le désir pour elle. La « Méditation » pour violon solo et orchestre, reliant les deux scènes de l'acte II, dépeint le début de la conversion de Thaïs.

Au départ, l'œuvre ne fut pas bien accueillie : en 1897, lorsque Sanderson se retira, elle n'en était qu'à sa quatorzième représentation. Mais la « Méditation » fut aussitôt un succès auprès des violonistes, et ses connotations religieuses encouragèrent en outre les organistes d'église à la jouer pendant la messe au moment de la communion. Même le *motu proprio* de 1903 du pape Pie X, qui demandait spécifiquement que la musique entendue à l'église « ne comportât pas de réminiscences de thèmes employés au théâtre d'opéra », ne put l'empêcher.

Sources

Il existe cinq sources :

S esquisses pour l'opéra (BN. Mus. Ms 4232 (I, II)) ; celles pour la « Méditation » se trouvent ff. 55–60.

A partition d'orchestre autographe (Opéra A. 665. a. I–IV Rés.) ; II, ff. 430–447.

EF première édition de la partition d'orchestre, Heugel, 1894, H. et Cie. 9434 (BN. Mus. Vm2 1029) ; pp. 277–289.

EV première édition de la réduction piano et chant, Heugel, 1894, H. et Cie. 7644 (BN. Mus. Vmb 33) ; pp. 127–131.

T transcription pour violon et piano de Martin Marsick, Heugel, 1894, H. et Cie. 9625 (1d).

Les esquisses (S) sont très proches de la version définitive. Dans la présente édition, les quelques variantes sont simplement notées comme autant de points intéressants.

La partition d'orchestre autographe (A) et la partition d'orchestre imprimée (EF) contiennent ensemble la plupart des principaux changements que j'ai faits pour établir la transcription (T). La réduction piano et chant (EV), étant donné qu'elle exige la compression de trois portées en deux, ne peut être considérée que comme une source secondaire. Outre qu'ils fournissent des doigtés et des marques de phrasé, de pédale et des indications verbales, A et EF proposent deux importantes modifications. Premièrement, Marsick a systématiquement supprimé la croche finale de harpe aux mesures 1–8, 11–16, etc. J'ai eu quelques scrupules à la rétablir, ne serait-ce que parce que, en 1894, Marsick et Massenet étaient collègues au Conservatoire et que la transcription de Marsick fut probablement soumise au compositeur. Mais la suppression de la croche produit un hoquet si laid dans la texture qu'il semblait préférable de suivre le texte de A et de EF (et EV), même si cela demande un peu d'agilité du pianiste. Deuxièmement, le retour de la mélodie à la mesure 40 et la coda à la mesure 59 sont accompagnés dans A et EF par un chœur à quatre voix qui chante doucement à bouche fermée, et dans les deux sources le compositeur note : « A défaut de voix, <u>les instruments à cordes joueront les petites notes</u>. » Il souhaitait manifestement un changement de couleur dans l'accompagnement à cet endroit. La présente édition comprend donc les parties vocales en petites notes aux mesures 40–47, puis de nouveau aux mesures 59–65, si bien que les pianistes peuvent faire ce changement de couleur s'ils le souhaitent.

Les coups d'archet et les doigtés de la partie de violon sont empruntés à A. Les indications de pédale aux mesures 13–18, 25–37, 51–55 et 68–71 sont de l'éditeur. Partout ailleurs, elles suivent T, à l'exception des passages notés dans le commentaire critique.

Roger Nichols

Traduction : Dennis Collins

VORWORT

Thaïs, Massenets zehnte vollendete Oper, hatte ihre Premiere an der Pariser Opéra am 16. März 1894 mit der amerikanischen Sopranistin Sibyl Sanderson in der Titelrolle. Das Libretto von Louis Gallet stützte sich auf Anatole Frances gleichnamigen Roman, der 1889 in der *Revue des deux mondes* als Fortsetzungsroman erschienen und im folgenden Jahr in Buchform herausgekommen war.

Erzählt wird die Geschichte von der Bekehrung der Kurtisane Thaïs zum Christentum durch einen heiligen Mann namens Athanaël (Paphnuce in Frances Roman) und von seiner gleichzeitigen, aber umgekehrten Bekehrung zu einem Leben, das vom Verlangen nach ihr beherrscht wird. Die »Méditation« für Solovioline und Orchester, welche die beiden Szenen des II. Akts verbindet, stellt den Beginn der Bekehrung Thaïs' dar.

Das Werk wurde anfangs nicht positiv aufgenommen: Als Sybil Sanderson 1897 in den Ruhestand trat, hatte es gerade erst seine vierzehnte Vorstellung erreicht. Dafür war die »Méditation« bei Violinisten ein unmittelbarer Erfolg, und ihre religiösen Anklänge bestärkten Kirchenorganisten darin, sie im Rahmen der Messe während der Kommunion zu spielen. Selbst das von Pius X. 1903 erlassene *motu proprio*, das ausdrücklich verlangte, daß Musik, die in der Kirche zu hören war, »keine Reminiszenzen an Themen aus dem Opernhaus« enthalten solle, konnte sich dagegen nicht durchsetzen.

Quellen

Es gibt insgesamt fünf Quellen:

S Skizzen zur Oper (BN. Mus. Ms 4232 (I, II)); die für die »Méditation« sind auf den Blättern 55–60 zu finden

A autographische Gesamtpartitur (Opéra A. 665. A. I–IV Rés.); II, Blätter 430–447

EF Erstausgabe der Gesamtpartitur, Heugel 1894, H. et Cie. 9434 (BN. Mus. Vm2 1029); Seiten 277–289

EV Erstausgabe der Gesangspartitur, Heugel 1894, H. et Cie. 7644 (BN. Mus. Vmb 33); Seiten 127–131

T Transkription von Martin Marsick für Violine und Klavier, Heugel 1894, H. et Cie. 9625 (1d).

Die Skizzen (S) kommen der Endfassung sehr nahe. In der vorliegenden Ausgabe sind die wenigen Abweichungen lediglich interessehalber vermerkt.

Die autographische Gesamtpartitur (A) und die gedruckte Gesamtpartitur (EF) enthalten zusammen die meisten Änderungen, die ich an der herkömmlichen Transkription (T) vorgenommen habe. Da die Gesangspartitur (EV) die Verdichtung von drei Notensystemen auf zwei erfordert, kann sie als Sekundärquelle betrachtet werden. A und EF liefern nicht nur Violingriffe, Phrasierung, Pedalangaben fürs Klavier und verbale Anweisungen, sondern legen auch zwei wesentliche Änderungen nahe. Erstens hat Marsick in den Takten 1–8, 11–16 usw. durchweg die letzte Achtelnote der Harfe gestrichen. Ich hatte einige Bedenken, sie wieder einzusetzen, nicht zuletzt deshalb, weil Marsick und Massenet 1894 Kollegen am Conservatoire waren und Marsicks Bearbeitung vermutlich unter der Aufsicht des Komponisten stattfand. Aber die Streichung des Achtels bringt einen so häßlichen Ruck ins Gefüge, daß es augenscheinlich vorzuziehen war, der Vorlage in A und EF (und EV) zu folgen, auch wenn dies vom Pianisten nur mäßige Fingerfertigkeit verlangt. Zweitens werden die Rückkehr der Melodie im Takt 40 und der Coda im Takt 59 in A und EF von einem vierstimmigen, leise summenden Chor begleitet, und in beiden Quellen lautet die Anweisung des Komponisten: »Wenn keine Gesangsstimmen zur Verfügung stehen, spielen Streichinstrumente die kleinen Noten.« Es ging ihm an dieser Stelle eindeutig um einen Wechsel der Klangfarbe in der Begleitung. Die vorliegende Ausgabe bezieht darum in den Takten 40–47 und noch einmal in den Takten 59–65 in Form von Stichnoten die Gesangsparts mit ein, damit der jeweilige Pianist nach Wunsch die Änderung vornehmen kann.

Bogenführung und Fingersatz im Violinpart sind A entnommen. Die Pedalangaben in den Takten 13–18, 25–37, 51–55 und 68–71 stammen vom Herausgeber. An allen anderen Stellen entsprechen sie den von T, außer dort, wo im Kritischen Kommentar Abweichungen vermerkt sind.

Roger Nichols

Übersetzung: Anne Steeb/Bernd Müller

Méditation

(Thaïs)

Jules Massenet
arr. Roger Nichols

Edition Peters No. 7510

JULES MASSENET

MÉDITATION

(Thaïs)

Violin and Piano

Edited and arranged by
Herausgegeben und bearbeitet von
Roger Nichols

Violin

EDITION PETERS

LONDON · FRANKFURT/M. · LEIPZIG · NEW YORK

Méditation

(Thaïs)

Jules Massenet
arr. Roger Nichols

Violin

Edition Peters No. 7510

Music-setting by Krystyna Reeder
Printed by Halstan & Co. Ltd, Amersham, Bucks., England

CRITICAL COMMENTARY

Bars 1–2, S, A, EF, EV, pf. These introductory bars not necessary, as previous music flows straight into bar 3. T has sustaining pedal lifted and replaced in bar 2; continuous string texture makes this redundant.

Bar 3, S has 'Lamento'. Vln, A marked 'bien chanté' instead of 'doux avec suavité'.

Bars 3–5, pf. T has sustaining pedal for each bar; see bars 1–2

Bars 7, 8, 10, 11, vln. Fingering and string indication from A, EF

Bar 11, pf. A has **pppp**

Bar 14, pf. ＜ starts on beat 3 in A; other sources, beat 2

Bars 16, 17, vln. Fingering and string indication from A, EF

Bar 17, vln. Notes 7, 8 tenuto markings from EV, T; absent in A, EF

Bars 19–20, pf. T has sustaining pedal lifted; see bars 1–2

Bars 22–38. A, EF have this part of tune played by orchestral first violins with soloist

Bar 22, vln. ⊓ from EF

Bars 22, 24, vln. S has quavers *c'*, *c'*, *a'*, *e'* and *e'*, *d'*, *c'♯*, *b'* respectively on beats 3 and 4; the idea of interlocking fourths was clearly a later addition

Bars 23, 24, vln. ＜ on final beats from EF

Bars 25, 28, 29, vln. Fingering and string indication from A, EF

Bars 26, 27, pf. RH held inner notes are closer to string texture of A, EF

Bar 28. A, EF marked **pppp**. EV marked 'calmato'. Pf LH notes 6–8 from A, EF; absent in T.

Bar 29, vln. 'dol.' from EV; S has triplet *g''*, *c''*, *f''* in beat 2. Pf LH note 7 *e'* from A, EF; T has *c'*

Bar 30, vln. *cresc.* on final quaver from A, EF; on beat 3 in T

Bar 32, vln. Notes 1, 2 tenuto markings from A, EF; absent in T

Bar 36, pf. LH text follows A, EF not T

Bar 38, pf. Spread chord (harp) from EV; not spread in T

Bar 39. Tune restored to solo violin in A, EF

Bars 40–47, pf. For small notes see Preface. A marked **pppp**; other sources **pp**.

Bars 40–42, pf. For pedalling, see bars 1–2, 3–5

Bars 44, 45, 47, 48, vln. Fingering from A, EF

Bar 48. Dynamic markings from A, EF; T has both parts **pp**. Pf, EV marked *una corda*

Bars 51–58. A, EF have this part of tune played by orchestral first violins with soloist

Bar 51, pf. ＜ absent in A

Bar 52, vln. EF has notes 3–6 phrased together; text follows A, T. See also bar 15 where all sources agree.

Bars 53–55, vln. Fingering and string indications from A, EF

Bar 54, vln. ＜ on beat 2 from A, EF; on beat 3 in T. See also bar 16 where all sources agree.

Bars 56–57, pf. T has sustaining pedal raised and replaced every half-bar; see bars 1–2, 3–5

Bar 58, pf. **pppp** from A, EF. Orchestral violins stop playing on tied *d'*.

Bars 59–65, pf. For small notes see Preface. I have retained the original disposition of these chords. In bars 59 and 60, pianists who cannot stretch the tenths are, of course, free to arrange their own voicings.

Bar 62, vln. Triplet marked 'dol.' and '(sans presser le groupe)' (without hurrying the triplet) in EV

Bars 64–71. In these final bars T makes its most radical departures from A, EF, in particular reversing the contributions of violin and accompaniment in bars 68 and 69. A, EF have been transcribed as faithfully as possible.

Bar 71, pf. Spread chord (harp) from EV; not spread in T

French Violin Music from Peters Edition

London • Frankfurt • Leipzig • New York

Debussy, C.

• Sonata (Garay) Urtext ....EP 9121

Fauré, G.

• Après un rêve (arr.Howat)..........................EP 7481

• Sicilienne Op.78 (Howat)..........................EP 7386

• Sonata No.1 in A Op.13..............................EP 7487
  Urtext (Howat)

• Sonata No.2 in E minor Op.108...............EP 9891a
  Urtext (Amerongen / Krebbers)

• Anthology of Original Pieces Urtext .....EP 7515
  (Howat) Berceuse Op.16; Morceau de lecture;
  Romance Op.28; Andante Op.75

Franck, C.

• Sonata in A (Jacobsen)..............................EP 3742

Ravel, M.

• Tzigane Urtext .... EP 10600
  (Thiemann / Kohlmann)

Saint-Saëns, C.

• Havanaise Op.83 Urtext ....EP 9292
  for Violin & Orchestra (Thiemann)

• Introduction and
  Rondo capriccioso Op.28.................... EP 9294
  (Bizet / Thiemann)

• Sonata in D minor Op.75 Urtext .. EP 9291
  (Thiemann)

Satie, E.

• 3 Gymnopédies (arr. Nichols)..........EP 7341

Classic Violin Studies and Tutors from Peters Edition

• **Basics**, by Simon Fischer.........................EP 7440
  300 exercises and practice routines to develop
  all aspects of violin technique

Casorti, A.

• Bowing Technique Op.50........................... EP 2516

Dancla, C.

• 50 Technical Studies Op.74......................EP 1080
  (Ecole du mécanisme)

• 20 Etudes brillantes Op.73.........................EP 1079

Dont, J.

• Etudes and Caprices Op.35...................... EP 3705
  (Jacobsen)

• 24 Preparatory Exercises Op.37..............EP 3706
  to Kreutzer & Rode Studies (rev. Sitt)

Fiorillo, F.

• 36 Studies (Caprices) (Davisson)..............EP 283a

Gavinies, P.

• 24 Etudes 'Matinées'.............................. EP 1381

Hrimaly, J.

• Scale Studies (Küchler)........................... EP 3879

Kayser, H.E.

• 36 Elementary and Progressive
  Studies Op.20 (Sitt).................................... EP 3560

Kreutzer, R.

• 42 Studies or Caprices (Hermann)............EP 284

• 42 Studies or Caprices (Hermann)............EP 284a
  2nd Violin part

• 42 Studies or Caprices (Davisson)...........EP 4310

Mazas, J-F.

• Studies Op.36
  Vol.1.. EP 1819a
  'Etudes spéciales', Studies Nos.1–30 (Davisson)
  Vol.2.. EP 1819b
  'Etudes brillantes', Studies Nos.31–57
  Vol.3.. EP 1819c
  Virtuoso Studies (Hermann)

Sitt, H.

• 50 Daily Exercises Op.98..........................EP 3122

Wieniawski, H.

• L'Ecole moderne Op.10 (Sitt)..................EP 3368

Wohlfahrt, H.

• 40 Elementary Studies Op.54 (Sitt)..........EP 3328

• 60 Studies Op.45 (Sitt)............................EP 3327

The ultimate compendium
of violin playing

London • Frankfurt • Leipzig • New York

Basics

by Simon Fischer
EP 7440

What is *Basics*?

Basics is the first complete guide to violin technique intended specifically for the music stand rather that the bookshelf. This unique publication covers all the fundamental aspects of playing the instrument. The 300 exercises and practice routines are grouped into seven highly detailed sections: right arm and hand, tone production, key strokes, left hand, shifting, intonation, vibrato.

By focusing on a single element at a time, each exercise is designed to achieve an immediately tangible and sustainable result in the shortest possible time. *Basics* is not a book to play through from cover to cover – after all, everybody's needs are different. The logical and uncluttered format enables the player to work directly on any specific technical matter that requires attention.

Who is *Basics* for?

For teachers

As well as presenting a wealth of original material, *Basics* also features ideas and principles traditionally associated with the great violinists, many of which have never been written down before. Some exercises are suitable for the youngest pupils, whilst others will benefit the most advanced players.
Always simple and direct, *Basics* offers powerful solutions to those common frustrations: awkwardness and tension, crooked bow, weak tone, poor intonation, vibrato problems etc.

For students

Nothing can replace a teacher, but this book will help you 'teach' yourself as you practise. Basics is a treasure trove of information and you are likely to be astonished how dramatic your development is.

For professional violinists

For the busy professional, *Basics* offers the most effective, least time-consuming method of maintaining the essentials: warm and even tone, reliable intonation, relaxed and versatile vibrato, freedom from tension etc.

Simon Fischer has emerged as one of the most acclaimed British violinists and teachers of his generation. He has appeared regularly as either soloist or guest leader with most of the leading national symphony and chamber orchestras, and has collaborated with such musicians as Yehudi Menuhin, André Previn and Vladimir Ashkenazy.

As a teacher, Simon Fischer's pedigree is equally impressive. He has achieved international prestige by virtue of his masterclasses for such organisations as ESTA, ASTA and ISM.

'Simon Fischer is a thoroughly accomplished violinist, a wonderful musician'
Vladimir Ashkenazy

'Original, detailed...useful to anyone sincerely concerned with violin technique.'
Dorothy DeLay on *Basics*